G000069583

A pint
and a prayer

reflections on daily life

kevin
mayhew

First published in 2006 by

KEVIN MAYHEW LTD
Buxhall, Stowmarket, Suffolk, IP14 3BW
E-mail: info@kevinmayhewltd.com
Website: www.kevinmayhew.com

9 8 7 6 5 4 3 2 1 0

ISBN 1 84417 519 7
Catalogue No. 1500880

Designed by Chris Coe

Printed and bound in China

Contents

Introduction

When the title **A Pint and a Prayer** was suggested to me,
I immediately warmed to it, yet not without certain reservations.
I was conscious, for one thing, that some would find any
association of alcohol and faith, however tenuous, offensive. I had
doubts also about the intended audience, which, initially, was
meant to be male. To me, that just didn't wash: a host of women
participate nowadays in what were previously seen as men's
activities, and vice versa, the days when gender could be
compartmentalised thankfully being long gone. Yet the idea implicit
in that title — namely, that faith and life should be inextricably
linked, and that prayer must touch people where they are rather
than be reserved for the religious few, continued to appeal; so
much so that I ended up writing three books rather than one, each
developing those twin convictions.

This book represents a selection from those three publications,
drawn together under that initially suggested title. Focusing on the
sort of things folk might talk about as they gather for a chat in their
local or over a meal — or indeed on the round of drinks or meal
itself! — it explores how everyday interests and pursuits can lead
naturally into prayer and reflection. My hope is that the prayers will
provide encouragement and inspiration to all those, male or female,
looking to relate the world of work and leisure to a living faith.

Nick Fawcett

The round of drinks

It was a round of drinks,
   nothing wrong with that,
   except that it was the last of many,
   and as a result one of those drinking
   would return home that night to beat his wife,
   another would brawl in the street,
   another sleep around,
   and another climb drunkenly into his car
   and mow down a passing pedestrian before veering off
   the road.

Teach us, Lord, to use rather than abuse your gifts,
   to enjoy them in moderation rather than excess.
And help us to understand that some must be handled with care,
   or else they will consume us instead of us them.

Amen.

The football match

He should have passed —
   one simple ball to the man in space,
   and a goal was all but certain.
He knew it,
   the fans knew it,
   but he'd carried on —
   brash and greedy,
   eyes only for personal glory —
   and the crowd groaned
   as he took on one player too many . . .
   and the chance was lost.

Lord, in pursuing personal goals and ambitions,
   teach me to think also of others,
   and, where necessary, to put their interests before my own.
Give me the humility I need to take a back seat sometimes,
   to play a supporting part,
   and to let others enjoy their moment.

Amen.

The car service

It wasn't anything complicated —
    just a change of oil, sparkplugs, air filter and so forth —
    but the impact was dramatic,
    as though my old banger had become a limousine,
    the engine steady,
    acceleration smooth,
    handling responsive.

Lord,
    overhaul my life,
    and make me new.
Recharge my batteries
    and clear away whatever chokes and undermines performance,
    preventing me from realising my true potential.
Remind me that you want me not just to get by
    but to live each moment to the full.

Amen.

The gym

They were a mixed bunch —
   some there on sufferance,
   fighting the flab,
   subjecting protesting bodies to unaccustomed exertion;
   others young and athletic,
   cultivating bulging biceps and body beautiful —
but they shared a common cause:
   the pursuit of physical health.

Lord,
   I don't want to neglect my body,
   for it is your gift,
   but what of my soul,
   the inner self?
Teach me to seek wholeness of spirit with equal resolve,
   to work for true well-being,
   to cultivate health that will neither fade nor perish.

Amen.

The production line

They came off the conveyor belt one after the other,
   hour after hour,
   day after day —
   the same process and same result,
   each a soulless copy of the one before,
   an automated clone.

As a society, Lord, we treat people the same way,
   seeing them as objects to be exploited,
   statistics processed,
   consumers targeted,
   resources managed.
Yet in **your** eyes we are all individuals
   unique and precious,
   valued for who we are.
Help us then, in all our dealings with others,
   to see behind the masks and labels,
   and to recognise the intrinsic worth of all.

Amen.

The DIY store

I walked among the shelves, Lord —
   row upon row of tools, machinery and equipment —
   and I thought of the stories each could one day tell:
   of skilled craftsmen surveying a job well done . . .
   and ham-fisted amateurs rueing a job botched;
   of homes improved . . .
   and houses ruined;
   of creative triumphs . . .
   and DIY disasters.

Lord, like everyone I can do **some** things by myself,
   but not all,
   for as well as strengths I have weaknesses,
   as well as skills, deficiencies.
Teach me, Lord, to know which is which:
   to tackle what I **can** do
   but admit to what I **can't**.

Amen.

The traffic lights

I put my foot down,
   determined to beat the lights,
   but they changed as I approached,
   forcing me to brake,
   and I cursed roundly,
   bemoaning my luck.

Why, Lord?
What did I hope to gain?
Why did I sour the moment I had in search of a few
   seconds more?
Grant me the gift of patience
   and the ability to celebrate the present,
   whatever it might bring.
Teach me to savour the here and now,
   and to let go of what may be or might have been.

Amen.

The wage packet

It spoke, Lord, that wage packet:
    of work done and leisure made possible,
    of food on the table and clothes for the kids,
    of presents, treats, holidays and outings,
    of the mortgage and new car,
    of taxes paid and pension contributions —
    all this and so much more.
It spoke too of those with no wage:
    the unemployed, asylum seekers, refugees,
    millions the world over condemned to poverty
    and a life of need.

I don't earn much, Lord —
    a mere pittance compared to some,
    but it's a king's ransom to others,
    riches beyond their wildest dreams.
So, then, however much I may strive for more,
    teach me first to appreciate what I have,
    and gratefully to respond to those with so much less.

Amen.

The new clothes

They fitted me well,
   the cut just what I was looking for,
   and I went out that day with a spring in my step,
   feeling good,
   smart,
   transformed.
But I wasn't, of course.
I was no different from the person I'd been before.
The clothes had changed, true,
   but I was just the same underneath as I'd always been.

You speak, Lord, of another kind of clothing –
   of gentleness, love, patience, humility, kindness and self-control.
Help me not just to toy with such garments,
   trying them on for a moment only to discard them afterwards,
   but to wear them each day –
   inner clothes that truly make a difference to who I am.

Amen.

The investment

I cashed the policy,
   frustrated by the lack of growth;
   then invested it again,
   seeking a better return,
   a higher yield for my cash.
And it seemed a shrewd move,
   for it swiftly grew,
   exceeding all expectations —
   a tidy nest egg for the years ahead.
Yet through whose hands did it pass to do so?
What activities did it finance,
   exploitation collude in
   and dubious dealings tacitly approve?

Lord, I mean no harm to anyone,
   my aim simply to put a little bit aside,
   but save me, in investing my money,
   from inadvertently selling my soul.

Amen.

The snooker player

He made it look so easy,
  rattling in one ball after another,
  and each time the next shot was lined up perfectly,
  the break accumulated with quiet but assured precision.
Only, of course, it **wasn't** easy;
  it was the result of years of discipline,
  countless days practising at the table,
  executing those seemingly effortless pots time after time,
  until a truly awesome skill became almost as natural as breathing.

Lord,
  give me similar commitment in following you,
  similar resolve to honour your will,
  similar dedication in discipleship.
Teach me truly to practise what I preach
  in the sense of working at doing so each day,
  until walking the way of Christ becomes second nature,
  not the exception but the norm.

Amen.

The radio

It was no good —
  despite all my efforts,
  all my tweaking,
  the signal was poor,
  hopelessly off the frequency,
  at best distorted,
  more often inaudible.

Lord, I find it just as hard to tune in to you.
Though you repeatedly speak —
  calling, teaching, confronting and encouraging —
  I get but a fraction of the message,
  the occasional snippet in what is otherwise a sea of noise.
Open my heart to you,
  that I may be more on your wavelength —
  receptive to your word,
  and responsive to your voice.

Amen.

The Internet

I went online, Lord,
   and all at once there was a world of information,
   incalculable resources at my fingertips,
   and into the bargain the opportunity to chat to friends,
   play games and share resources,
   to learn, talk and interact with people and places across the globe.

I went online again,
   and suddenly there was a world of corruption:
   sickening and vile pornography,
   images of violence and incitements to hatred,
   perverts grooming their prey
   and scams targeting the unwary —
   the pimp, torturer, child molester and conman welcomed into my
   living room.

Lord, it disturbs me, the Internet,
   for it's too much like me,
   too much like all of us,
   capable of so much good
   yet so much evil,
   so much beauty
   yet so much ugliness.
Nurture whatever enriches,
   whatever builds up,
   and purge that which demeans and degrades your creation
   in any part.

Amen.

The eBay auction

They waited before making their bids,
    each anxious to pay as little as possible to secure their prize,
    and then, as the price rose,
    one by one,
    they fell away,
    the cost too high to stomach.

With you, Lord, it's a different story.
Though I am worth so little, you were willing to give your all,
    gladly and without reserve,
    no price too high or cost too great to make **me** yours
    and **you** mine.
For that awesome truth
    and amazing love,
    thank you.

Amen.

The fisherman

He'd been there for hours,
  sprawled on the bank,
  occasionally stirring to re-bait his hook
  and cast off once more.
No rush,
  no bustle,
  seemingly with all the time in the world.
Then . . .
  suddenly . . .
  a nibble,
  a tug on the line,
  and he was up,
  reeling in his catch —
  another successful day's fishing.

Lord,
  I'm not so good at waiting.
I like to see speedy results,
  instant returns,
  and when plans are frustrated,
  rewards delayed,
  I fret and sulk.
I'm not good at waiting for **you** either,
  angry when prayers go unanswered,
  requests apparently unheeded.
Remind me that the best things come to those who wait,
  and teach me to do things not in **my** time
  but in **yours**.

Amen.

The rugby team

His team-mates engulfed him,
  leaping and laughing,
  sharing his jubilation as he punched the air in triumph,
  delight on his face.
The try was his,
  but the moment was owned by all,
  for each had contributed,
  if not in the move itself then in the play earlier.
The clever shimmy,
  last-ditch tackle,
  defence-splitting pass,
  bruising scrum —
  each had added to the whole,
  the game not about one but many.

Teach me, Lord, that I need others,
  just as they need me;
  that life is interconnected,
  what I owe balanced by what I can contribute.
Whether I'm the centre of attention or unnoticed,
  help me to play my part,
  working both **with** and **for** others
  to the common good.

Amen.

The computer game

I was in control —
   able to shape lives,
   move armies,
   fashion empires,
   influence history —
   and it was compelling stuff,
   addictive,
   like crafting a new world . . .
   playing God.

Only, of course, I **wasn't** in control, Lord,
   not in the real world,
   I being no more able to dictate my destiny
   than to create life or defy death,
   such a feat beyond my reach.
I can shape things, to a point,
   exert influence for better or worse,
   but more often than not **I'm** the one being shaped,
   swept along by the latest current of opinion or tide of events.
Teach me where true power really lies:
   not in **my** hands
   but in **yours**.

Amen.

The darts match

The crowd waited expectantly as he took aim,
    then sent the dart spiralling towards the board:
    another triple twenty,
    another maximum score.
He'd set his sights high,
    consistently targeting the top –
    and the strategy reaped handsome rewards.

When it comes to discipleship, Lord,
    for all my talk of commitment and sacrificial service
    I set my sights low,
    content to get by rather than excel.
Forgive my limited aspirations and weakness of resolve,
    and help me to aim higher,
    targeting a deeper faith and fuller response to your love –
    a life more closely lived with you.

Amen.

The carpenter

I watched spellbound as he worked:
   taking the rough-hewn block of wood
   and turning it on the lathe,
   sculpting and shaping it with gouge and chisel,
   painstakingly transforming the ordinary into a work of art.

And I thought, Lord, of the carpenter's son,
   learning his trade in Nazareth;
   of **your** Son,
   nailed to a rough-hewn cross;
   of the young man leaving his father's workshop
   to build instead his Father's kingdom,
   fashioning not just timber but human lives.

Fashion me now, Lord, by the touch of your hand,
   and finish your new creation.
Take who I am,
   and from the deadwood of my life
   craft something beautiful for you.

Amen.

The cricket match

It was a difficult time to come in:
    a massive score to chase
    and wickets having tumbled,
    carelessly tossed away.
One false stroke could have spelt disaster,
    not just for him but also for the team.
But he got his head down,
    dug in
    and ground out a score,
    only cutting loose when the game was safe,
    his determined concentration turning defeat into victory,
    failure into success.

Teach me, Lord, there is a time and place for everything:
    for action . . . and restraint,
    for taking risks . . . and showing caution,
    for enthusiasm . . . and patience,
    for abandonment . . . and self-discipline.
Help me to know which is which,
    and to get the balance right.

Amen.

The football scarf

He wore it with pride,
  happy to be associated with his team,
  their trials and disappointments,
  victories and defeats,
  the scarf being more than an item of clothing —
  a way rather of identifying himself with the players,
  displaying his allegiance to all.

Am I proud, Lord, to be linked with **you**,
  ready in turn to show where my loyalties lie?
Or am I a closet disciple,
  hiding my faith away for fear of what others might think,
  should they know where I truly stand?
Teach me never to be ashamed of you,
  lest the day come when I find **you** ashamed of **me**.

Amen.

The sports star

He had it all —
 fast car, swanky house, luxury lifestyle —
 but it wasn't simply down to luck.
He was gifted, yes,
 far more than many,
 but he'd honed his skills through patient practice,
 years of hard work belying the apparent ease with which
 he played.

My gifts are less eye-catching, Lord,
 never destined to turn heads or win plaudits,
 but they're gifts nonetheless,
 held in trust for you.
Help me to make the most of them
 and to use them not just for my benefit
 but for others too,
 consecrating all I am and all I do to your service.

Amen.

The bookmakers

They have it right most of the time,
   experience having taught them to weigh up the odds
   and adjust them as necessary,
   but,
   just occasionally,
   a rank outsider springs a surprise,
   coming through to take the prize.

Remind me, Lord, that you are a God of surprises,
   constantly overturning the expectations of this world,
   turning weakness to strength,
   despair to hope
   and defeat to victory.
Teach me, then,
   however much I feel up against it,
   however daunting the challenge and feeble my resources,
   to trust in you,
   knowing that nothing finally will be able to frustrate your will
   or deny the triumph of your love.

   Amen.

The tug of war

It looked easy at the beginning
    as the two teams took the strain,
    each gritting their teeth and digging in,
    but once battle began in earnest, it all changed:
    faces purple with effort,
    sweat dripping from fevered brows,
    tired legs buckling and muscles stretched to the limit
    as a few feet were won,
    only to be lost again.

For all my talk, Lord, of closeness,
    the relationship between us is more like a tug of war than
    shared embrace,
    a broken marriage than match made in heaven,
    for, despite my best intentions,
    I constantly pull away from you,
    resisting your will
    and attempting to impose mine in its place.
Teach me that, however hard I strive against you,
    you will never let go,
    and so may I learn to work **with** you instead.

Amen.

The garden

I sowed,
   planted,
   weeded,
   pruned,
   and watched in delight as bloom followed bloom
   in a vibrant fusion of fragrance and colour.

The labour was mine, Lord,
   but the creation yours,
   for it is your hands that fashion such beauty
   and sustain life itself.
Teach me to work in partnership with you,
   not just in the world of plants
   but in that of everyday life and relationships,
   seeking to nurture the full potential of everyone
   and everything.

Amen.

The joke

It wasn't side-splittingly funny,
    but it was enough to raise the spirits —
    bringing a smile in place of a frown
    and offering a welcome reminder of the funny side of life.

Though much in life, Lord, is touched by pathos,
    teach me to keep a sense of humour,
    able to laugh, even through tears,
    and smile, even in sorrow.
And though much is serious,
    demanding a measured response and sober judgement,
    help me to retain a sense of fun,
    aware that laughter is your gift,
    as valuable and special as any.

Amen.

The golf shot

I caught it well,
  better than expected,
  and it soared through the air,
  overshooting the green by a mile
  and landing in the undergrowth beyond.
It had been the wrong club –
  a long iron when a wedge would have done the job –
  and the result was an unplayable lie.

Teach me, Lord, to recognise my strengths and weaknesses,
  those things I'm made for and those I'm not,
  and teach me equally to respect the qualities of others,
  open to what they can do that I can't.

Amen.

The surfers

I watched them riding the waves,
   their exhilaration plain
   as, in glorious harmony with the elements,
   they ducked, dived, twisted and turned,
   and I marvelled at the beauty and grandeur of creation,
   its power to uplift the body and transport the spirit,
   wonderful beyond words.
But I couldn't help recalling other waves,
   destructive and terrifying,
   engulfing homes,
   obliterating communities —
   a merciless torrent overwhelming countless lives —
   and I marvelled at the savagery of creation,
   its power to **crush** the body and **shatter** the spirit,
   dreadful beyond words.

Why, Lord, did you create a world so awesome yet so awful,
   enriched by joy yet cursed by sorrow;
   a world in which so much speaks of your care,
   but so much else denies it,
   giving your love the lie?
Help me to wrestle honestly with the good and bad,
   the best and the worst in life,
   and somehow to make sense of you in each.

Amen.